DEDICATION

To my husband, Evan, for believing in me.
To our children, Rayna, Sari, Eli and Arin,
for encouraging and inspiring me.

Read this When…

Empowering Messages for Powerless Moments

Alice Langholt, MJS

ISBN: 1514728508
ISBN-13: 978-1514728505

CONTENTS

FOREWORD

Tragedies in the world, financial struggles, and personal crises can leave us feeling outraged, angry, grief-stricken, and most of all, powerless. The situations that produce these powerless moments are usually beyond our control.

Let this full-color book of empowering messages and beautiful graphics inspire you and help restore your optimism when you need it most.

For example:

- The news delivers stories of violence, hatred, and tragedy. Murder, rioting, looting, and destruction are presented in abundance in the news and social media sources daily.

- There are articles proclaiming that our food and water are unsafe, tainted, or making us sick. We hear that our elected officials have voted to support organizations that are withholding information from us about the ingredients in our food or its origins. Then, we read that the pharmaceutical companies are benefitting from creating drugs for treating symptoms instead of finding cures. Fear, frustration, and mistrust pervade our lives all the time.

- Work life can be another source of powerless feelings, as we juggle office politics, money struggles, and trying to please everyone while striving for work-life balance.

- Home life can also be overwhelming, overloaded with responsibilities, expectations, demands, children, teens, hormones, drama, arguments, enforcing rules, and trying to find time for ourselves.

- People can be mean. People can be thoughtless, condescending, rude, selfish, and insensitive. We can too. And then we feel crappy about it.

- People we love get sick, have accidents, and sometimes die. Or we get sick, have accidents, and might die sooner than we had expected. It seems unfair.

Powerless moments can feel overwhelming. These moments hurt. We often react to them by experiencing even more emotions: despair, frustration, anger, and hopelessness.

I noticed that when I'm experiencing one of those moments, writing a message to myself helps me feel more empowered. Sometimes the message is a prayer to my Higher Wisdom, or a poem, or a series of affirmations. Sometimes I've liked what I've written enough to make it into a graphic and post it on my Facebook wall.

After a while of doing this, I had a little collection of them. So, I started putting them into categories organized by what powerless feeling I was trying to change by writing that particular message. I realized that the writings were becoming something cohesive; a little guide to choose an empowering message based on the situation I was facing in the moment.

That's how this book emerged.

It is my hope that this book will be useful for you, and become a source of empowerment when you are facing a powerless moment.

I hope that when you're feeling powerless, or any of the unpleasant emotions that often follow, that you'll pick up this book, identify how you feel, and read something that speaks to you in such a way that your powerless feeling is replaced by something better.

I also hope that this book will inspire you to write some empowering messages of your own when you're feeling powerless.

Thank you for sharing my words.
Alice

HOW TO USE THIS BOOK

1. Turn back to the Contents page.

2. Select the situation that is closest to how you are feeling.

3. Turn to the page designated for that situation and read the empowering message(s) in that section.

4. Let the message speak to you.

Repeat as needed.

READ THIS WHEN…

WHEN THE NEWS IS ATROCIOUS

Inner Wisdom, Guide me:

To find my connection to the Source of Love
When outside myself it seems missing.

To know that I can still offer goodness
When others are not.

To choose gratitude
Over frustration.

And to bring peace
To my corner of the world.

Thank you.

The collective consciousness is teeming with:
Indignant outrage,
Righteous ranting,
Anger-fueled arguments,
Spotlights pointed on injustice,
Blatant disregard for life,
Intentional cruelty and hate
Around the world
And around the block.

Fear is pumped into
The channels of information
We tap into for our connection to reality.

It's time to change the ingredients;
To temper the molecular makeup
Of the mental and emotional flow
That our life force energy is bathing in 24-7.

It's time to join with the others around the globe
Who are sharing the same mission –
To dilute the pollution
Until it's no longer potent.

Take a few minutes to intentionally connect with their current
of thoughts,
And offer these up in a flowing stream:
Seconds of stillness,
Pauses of peace,
Compassion-filled breaths,
Reminders of love,
The grace of gratitude.

And together we'll shift the energy of the world
Towards the light.

Whatever we give attention to
grows stronger.
Today I will give my attention to :

Words of love and kindness

Messages that make my soul sing

Pictures that inspire me

People doing good in the world

Positive people

Thoughts and expressions of gratitude

Beautiful music

Healing energy

Adding light to the world

WHEN YOU FEEL INADEQUATE

The tiniest spark
Makes the darkness recede.

A caring presence,
The words, "I'm listening,"
Compassionate silence,
A thoughtful gesture without expectation.

A spark isn't just an insignificant thing.
It carries the capacity to ignite,
To inspire more sparks,
And then, kindle a flame.

This small flame is
Warmth,
Love,
Healing,
And contains the energy
That transmutes hopelessness
Into promise.

My Prayer

Please help me use the gifts I've been given to lighten the way for others.

Please show me ways to strengthen my gifts to make the most of my journey, for myself, and all I can best serve.

Please send to me those who I'm here to help, and those who can show me how to shine my light brighter.

Please allow me to make a difference in the world so that I leave it better for having been here.

Amen

We are all saviors of
humankind

If we accept the
challenge

to do what
we can do

for others

for ourselves

and for our planet.

WHEN PEOPLE ARE MEAN

It's not up to me
To control your actions,
To change your mind,
To choose your words.

Wishing and waiting
For a change from you
Will not make it happen.

But I can choose
What I'll accept,
What I'll let upset me,
What I'll allow into my heart.

And I can decide
To measure my worth
By the infinite flow of love
That makes up my soul,
Allowing only that which harmonizes
With this frequency
To share my song.

Cruelty is a defensive action.
It is fueled by fear:
   Fear of having no power.
   Fear of being inadequate.

Fear is healed by love:
   Love of self.
   Love that nurtures.
   Love that reassures.
Love that affirms that everyone
Without exception
Is worthy of an infinite measure of love.

First, let it in for yourself.
Allow love
   to fill your being,
      nurture, reassure,
         and affirm your worthiness.

Then, offer the overflow to those who need it.

If some are not ready to accept this love,
Send it to them in thoughts, whispers, and prayers.

And then, go out and offer love to those who are ready.
You'll know them because they are overflowing with their own,
And are offering it back to you.

WHEN YOU'RE STUCK IN A RUT

Here's what the School of Hard Knocks didn't teach you:
You don't need to know how to get what you want.

The "how" will take care of itself
When you know **what** you want.

Focus on letting your imagination run free.
Let it take you to the visions
that show you what it would be like:
  to experience joy
  to be at your best
  to know you are engaged in your soul's calling.

Imagine it deeply,
Until you are breathing in the sense of joy and relief
That comes from knowing you are immersed
in the Divine Flow of Life.

Don't worry that it's "just imagination,
Or "only thoughts, nothing more."

The imagination is a powerful Creator.
The engine of change is fueled by creative thought.

You don't need to know the specifics.
You just need to know how it feels to have them.
The fuel of opportunity is enriched by joy and gratitude,
So be liberal with that stuff.

And when the skateboard, go-cart, pickup,
Or train of opportunity
Comes along offering you a ride, jump aboard.

Be ready to align a wheel, change a spark plug,
Or pull the whistle.
Get your hands full of grease
As you gain momentum
On the journey
of becoming who you were born to be.

First, a dream.

Pause to add fuel:
Anticipation,
  enthusiasm,
    excitement,
and a dash of *why the hell not,*
topped off with a splash of gratitude.

Energy is flowing,
Creation is in motion.

Pieces start to manifest,
and fly for assembly
into the waiting hands of the dreamer.

WHEN THINGS DON'T WORK OUT
AS YOU HAD PLANNED

It's natural to be pissed off.
You're disappointed? Understandable.
Many in your shoes would think
That they've been cheated by the world.

You wanted it. You reached for it.
And yet, it didn't happen.
Embarrassed, self-confidence lost,
You're hurt, rejected, and upset.

Take a deep breath,
Then say two words to turn it all around,
To point you in a new direction
To gain a renewed motivation.

Successful people say these words,
For "Failure" is just another step.
It's a label to let go of,
And a chance to reassess.

These words will free you.
You will take control
And start to move ahead.

They form a two-word question.
First you ask,
Then answer it.

Are you ready?
Say them now.
The words to say are,
"What's next?"

WHEN THINGS
DON'T WORK
OUT AS YOU
HAD PLANNED,

IT'S BECAUSE
YOUR NEXT
IDEA IS
BETTER.

WHEN SOMEONE YOU LOVE DIES

A river is joined by various streams
As it goes along its path.
Each stream brings with it
Particles of all its touched along the way:

Lessons and wisdom from stones, mud and tadpoles.
Memories of storms, white waters,
            and the musings of minnows.
Whispers from reeds and softness of cattails.
Leaves infused with sunshine from the treetops,
And pebbles tossed along with the laughing current.

The waters merge and then diverge again.
Each are changed from experiencing the other.
Each enriched, made more complex,
Each stream grows more intricate from this interaction.

So it is our lives are changed by those we touch.
However briefly,
The encounter shifts us,
And we always carry something more
Because our paths have merged.

"My life won't ever be the same."
That's true.
It doesn't have to.
It isn't meant to.

Making a difference is part of living a life of meaning.

Leaving a void means something was there that mattered.

What a blessing.

Sit with the blessing of this person's life.
Bring it into your heart and let it become a sacred part of you.

And know that you are carrying it forth
As your life continues on from here,
Wiser, more loving, and more grateful for each moment.

WHEN LIFE FEELS UNFAIR

Let me connect with
my Higher Wisdom
That knows the lesson
hiding deep within the seeds of this experience.

Let me remove
The hard outer husks,
The prickles and thorns,
The scratching brambles of stems,

To find the kernels of truth,
The hidden small fears
That were protected
By the stories I told myself –

The beliefs I've formed,
Tended, and clung to
And sorted into columns labeled "right" and "wrong."

Let me hold those small seeds,
Now unprotected,
And nurture them with kindness,
Feed them with compassion, forgiveness,
And healing light,

To transform them –
Help them grow healthy, green and lush.

Higher Wisdom,
Gently restrain me from planting more spiky weeds,
For lessons untended will multiply
Until the garden is overtaken.

Let me tend these seeds,
And as they are pruned, cleaned, and planted again,
Let the garden of my life
Sprout blooms of gratitude, blessings,
And fruits of abundance.

A Recipe for Abundance

6 Cups of Good Things You Already Have
1 teaspoon Essence of Joy
3 Cups of Gratitude

Directions:
Sift the Good Things, and carefully rub each one with a pinch of Essence of Joy.

Stir in the Gratitude to fully incorporate.

Place into a large 12 cup capacity saucepan. Warm on the stove over low heat, stirring to release the full aromas.

As it is stirred, notice that it will gradually increase in volume until the pan is overflowing.

Enjoy with family and friends.

WHEN YOU NEED A FRESH PERSPECTIVE

Just suppose that we live many lifetimes.
Can you wrap your mind around that
For the sake of this exercise?

If we do live many lifetimes,
That means that this one could be designated as
Your best one ever.

If that were the case,
Would you spend your time
   Consumed by self-doubt
   Beating yourself up
   Swept into everyone else's drama?

Or would you
   Take every opportunity to live life to the fullest?
   Love as deeply as you could?
   Connect, create, and explore the reach of your potential?

Suppose your other lifetimes are destined to fall short in
terms of joy, pleasure, peace and love,
Compared with this one.

Would you make more of an effort to find the joy in every
moment
And be grateful for the blessings they hold?

Other lifetimes may involve you fleeing war,
Or suffering from disease,
Powerless, oppressed, in pain,
Or scrounging for a meal.

But, this one,
This one is a gift,
A pause
A sweet reprieve.
It's a call to hold each precious moment sacred.

Can you open up
Your heart and soul and eyes
To see abundant blessings
Filling up your days?

Can you gaze through eyes of compassion,
Choosing to be slow to judge
And quick to love?

This lifetime
It could be your easiest one.
The next one might be painful, harder,
It may hold labored, anguished lessons.

If you knew that now,
How would that change the way
  You savor every second?
  You respond to little crises?
  You invest your heart in everything you offer?
  You learn, and love?

How would it change the ways
You add your unique signature
To the world?

We are all

unique as a snowflake

made of the same atomic materials
as each other, and as the stars

individual in thought, emotion,
and history

interacting every millisecond
with air, water, fire, and earth

contributing our thoughts,
dreams, and love
to the global consciousness

Mountains	Streams	Infants
Rivers	Whispers	Bird songs
Trees	Sighs	Raindrops
Clovers	Caresses	Crickets
Ants	Nurturing	Moonbeams
Lions	Berries	Rainbows
Mammoths	Inspirations	Giggles
Kittens	Smiles	Teardrops
Clouds	Friends	Dog licks
Pebbles	Daydreams	Cat purrs
Blood cells	Wishes	Harmonies
Breathing	Singing	Ocean waves
Heartbeats	Painting	Sunshine
Kindness	Dancing	Stars
Compassion	Surprises	Dreams
Hugs	Sand grains	Prayers
Love	Minnows	Epiphanies
Kisses	Butterflies	Forgiveness
Cows	Silence	Poetry

HOLY

WHEN YOU'RE LOSING FAITH
IN HUMANITY

It's bad out there.
But I've got a warm, beating heart
That shows me visions of a better place.

There's fighting out there.
But I've got two hands reaching out
To hold someone close to me.

There's violence out there.
But I've got two sensitive eyes
Seeking out the goodness in the world.

There's hatred out there.
But I've got peace in my space
To welcome all with love and acceptance.

There's hopelessness out there.
But I've got a voice
To impart words of comfort and assurance to all.

You know that wish you have inside,
The one of how you want the world to be?

The vision of a world full of peaceful interactions,
People helping each other,
And where food, air, water, and shelter
Are safe and plentiful?

Where children are raised to be kind,
Success is assured for accomplishing your soul's purpose,
And everyone has what they need
to become who they're meant to be?

Don't give up on it.

All of your dreams, efforts, actions
And persistence in believing it can happen
Turn the wheel a little more
In the direction of creation.

WHEN YOU FEEL OVERWHELMED

The day goes on.
The work gets done.
Tomorrow will follow again.

Take a breath.
There's time for that.
Take a few more.
You can allow it.

You're capable.
You've got this.
The power's in your hands.

Do what you can.
That's all that's asked.
Ultimately, you decide
What and how much
That will be.

What if?
What if you said, "No" this time?
What if you let someone else help?
What if you moved something onto tomorrow's list?

What if
   you
      just
         didn't
            get
              it
                all
                  done?

Would the world end?
Would your life end?
Would someone be disappointed?
Would that person survive the disappointment?

Or would you just get it done tomorrow instead?

WHEN YOU FEEL DISCONNECTED

The network of tree roots
Communicates with other trees and plants
Across the forest.
This communication system
Helps the trees share nutrients with each other
To keep them all balanced.

Just like the trees,
We are all connected.
If you are joyful,
Share some up to the grid of life.

If you are hurting,
Ask to receive some soothing and peace –
It's waiting for you.

Be a tree.
Send your roots down.
Plug into the soil's power grid.
Absorb Mother Earth's healing vibrations.

Trace their path up your trunk
To replenish your heart
With the promise of growth,
Moss, clay, and crystals,
Nutrient-dense, and pulsing with life.

Send your branches way, way up.
Steep your leaves in the Sun's restorative light.
Draw the light deep into your soul.

The infinite supply of love and energy
Is there for all life.
There are no prerequisites, no conditions.
You're alive? You're invited.
Tap in, and receive all you need.

Look up at the sky.

Everyone on the planet sees it,
But it looks different from every person's vantage point.

To see the whole sky,
Take everyone's view
Combined together.
Or, better yet, don't.
A view like that
Is too much for one person to process.

Instead, get real close to someone.
Look up together,
And tell each other everything you see in detail.

That size of the sky
is the perfect view.

ALICE LANGHOLT

ABOUT THE AUTHOR

 Alice Langholt is the founder and Executive Director of Reiki Awakening Academy School of Intuitive Development (ReikiAwakeningAcademy.com). Her other books include the award winning book, *Practical Reiki: for balance, well-being, and vibrant health. A guide to a simple, revolutionary energy healing method* and *The Practical Reiki Companion* workbook. She is also the author of a series of books, cards, and products for busy people, which focus on 30 second methods of self-care, including: *A Moment for Mom, A Moment for Us, A Moment for Success,* and the A Moment for Me 365 Day Calendar. Find them at amoment4me.com. She has also published a work of fiction entitled *First Family*.

Alice is a wife and mother of four children and lives in the Washington, DC metro area.

See her author website at AliceLangholt.com.

Did you like this book? Please leave a review on Amazon.com or GoodReads.com.

Made in the USA
Middletown, DE
23 April 2022